CRAYOLA COLOR IN CULTURE

Mari Schuh

Lerner Publications ◆ Minneapolis

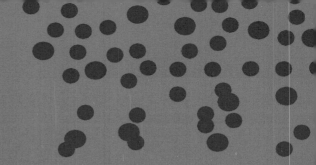

TO FAIRMONT ELEMENTARY SCHOOL

Official Licensed Product
Lerner Publications Company
A division of Lerner Publishing Group, Inc.
241 First Avenue North
Minneapolis, MN 55401 USA

For reading levels and more information, look up this title at www.lernerbooks.com.

Main body text set in Billy Infant Regular 24/40.
Typeface provided by SparkyType.

Library of Congress Cataloging-in-Publication Data

Names: Schuh, Mari C., 1975– author.
Title: Crayola color in culture / by Mari Schuh.
Description: Minneapolis : Lerner Publications, 2018. | Series: Crayola colorology | Includes bibliographical references and index.
Identifiers: LCCN 2017018466 (print) | LCCN 2017043334 (ebook) | ISBN 9781512497731 (eb pdf) | ISBN 9781512466898 (lb : alk. paper) | ISBN 9781541511637 (pb : alk. paper)
Subjects: LCSH: Color—Social aspects—Juvenile literature. | Color in design—Juvenile literature. | Color in clothing—Juvenile literature. | Crayons—Juvenile literature.
Classification: LCC QC495.5 (ebook) | LCC QC495.5 .S3686 2018 (print) | DDC 535.6—dc23

LC record available at https://lccn.loc.gov/2017018466

Manufactured in the United States of America
2-47053-32454-12/20/2018

TABLE OF CONTENTS

AMAZING COLORS

The world is full of colors. Color is part of culture.

Culture is the art we make, the clothes we wear, and the way we live in the world.

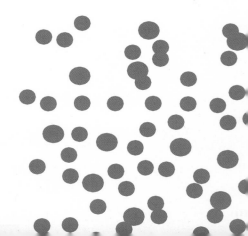

WE WEAR COLORS!

We wear colors every day.

You might wear team or school colors.

Or you can wear your favorite color.

How do you choose the colors you wear?

Some colors and styles of clothing remind us of countries and cultures.

Colored bracelets are popular in India.
These colorful hats come from Morocco.

People wear different colors around the world.

Colors can help us remember a country's history.

In Mexico, green is the color of freedom.

This woman in Peru wears a colorful shawl. What colors do you see?

CELEBRATING WITH COLOR

Colors help us celebrate.

People celebrate Holi in India, Nepal, and in many other countries.

Holi is the festival of colors.

In spring, many people decorate Easter eggs.

Brightly colored eggs remind us of nature and new life.

Red is used to celebrate the Chinese New Year.

Red means good luck.

A COLORFUL WORLD

Countries have colors too.

Greece's flag is blue and white.

Blue is the color of the sea and sky.

White is the color of clouds.

We use colors to decorate our homes.

These colorful cloth plates come from Ethiopia.

THE MEANING OF COLOR

In India, blue is a very special color. It is the color of a god named Krishna.

People all around the world celebrate Day of the Dead with many colors. On this day, purple shows sadness, and white means hope.

Colorful skulls decorate Day of the Dead.

Weddings are a special time. People use many colors to celebrate.

Red is a popular color in Chinese and Indian weddings. Red stands for happiness, love, and beauty.

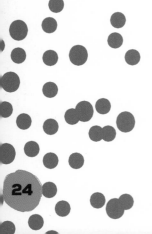

Colors are full of meaning. They help us celebrate, and they decorate our world.

What do colors mean to you?

MANY COLORS

Colors are all around the world.

Find these Crayola® colors in the photos.

Blush

Razzmatazz

Inchworm

Granny Smith Apple

Carnation Pink

Cadet Blue

Wild Strawberry

Goldenrod

GLOSSARY

Chinese New Year: an important Chinese holiday that starts on the first day of the year on the Chinese calendar

culture: the way of life of a group of people

Day of the Dead: a holiday celebrated around the world that honors life and family

history: past events

Holi: a holiday to celebrate spring

nature: the world of living things and the outdoors

symbols: things that stand for something else

TO LEARN MORE

BOOKS

Cantillo, Oscar. *Blue around Me*. New York: Cavendish Square, 2015.
   Explore the color blue by reading about all the places it can be found.

Schuh, Mari. *Crayola Science of Color*. Minneapolis: Lerner Publications, 2018.
   Learn how we see color and how colors blend together to make different colors.

Sebra, Richard. *It's Easter!* Minneapolis: Lerner Publications, 2017.
   Read about colorful Easter symbols such as eggs, flowers, and food.

WEBSITES

Chinese New Year
   https://www.education.com/worksheets/chinese-new-year/
   Complete worksheets to better understand Chinese New Year.

National Geographic Kids: **Day of the Dead**
   http://kids.nationalgeographic.com/explore/celebrations/day-of-the-dead/
   Learn more about this very colorful holiday.

What Colors Mean
   https://www.factmonster.com/features/speaking-language/what-colors
   -mean
   This website explains the many meanings of color.

INDEX

PHOTO ACKNOWLEDGMENTS

The images in this book are used with the permission of: © RoyStudioEU/Shutterstock.com (linen background throughout); © Nila Newsom/Dreamstime.com, p. 5 (top); © Sebikus/Dreamstime.com, p. 5 (bottom); Crystal Kirk/Shutterstock.com, p. 7 (top left); © Kameel4u/Dreamstime.com, p. 7 (top right); iStock.com/ERphotographer, p. 7 (bottom left); © Monkey Business Images/Dreamstime.com, p. 7 (bottom right); Nagarjun Kandukuru/flickr.com (CC BY 2.0), p. 7 (center); © Nikhil Gangavane/Dreamstime.com, pp. 9 (top), 28 (top left); © Maciej Czekajewski/Dreamstime.com, p. 9 (bottom); CHRISTIAN DE ARAUJO/Shutterstock.com, p. 11 (top); Bartosz Hadyniak/E+/Getty Images, p. 11 (bottom); Poras Chaudhary/Stone/Getty Images, p. 13 (top); iStock.com/Intellistudies, p. 13 (bottom); © Redbaron/Dreamstime.com, p. 15; P_Wei/E+/Getty Images, p. 17 (top); View Stock/Getty Images, p. 17 (bottom); Samot/Shutterstock.com, p. 19; iStock.com/mtcurado, p. 21; Shyamalamuralinath/Shutterstock.com, p. 23 (top); iStock.com/agustavop, p. 23 (bottom); iStock.com/gooddesign10, p. 25 (top left); shuige/Moment/Getty Images, p. 25 (bottom left); IVY PHOTOS/Shutterstock.com, p. 25 (right); iStock.com/huePhotography, p. 27; iStock.com/StevanZZ, p. 28 (bottom left); © Harun/Dreamstime.com, p. 28 (top right).

Cover: iStock.com/THEPALMER (Holi festival); iStock.com/StevanZZ (houses); © Giuseppe Esposito/Dreamstime.com (toys); © Nikhil Gangavane/Dreamstime.com (lanterns); RoyStudioEU/Shutterstock.com (linen texture background); TairA/Shutterstock.com (watercolor background).

LERNER
e
SOURCE™

Expand learning beyond the printed book. Download free, complementary educational resources for this book from our website, www.lernerresource.com.